CPP/Belwin presents . . .

Henry Mancini

GREATEST HITS

D1571449

KORG PORTRAITS

Henry Mancini
Concert Pianos

With 18 Oscar nominations, four Academy Awards and a host of chart-topping albums to his credit, Henry Mancini's remarkably successful career as a composer and instrumentalist speaks for itself. But when it comes to Korg Concert Pianos, we let Henry do the talking.

"The sound and feeling of the Concert Piano gives me the satisfaction of an acoustic piano. But it also gives me a lot more sounds to play with in a practical and compact format."

For more information about KORG CONCERT PIANOS, please write to KORG U.S.A., 89 Frost Street Westbury, NY 11590

ISBN 0-89898-717-2

9 780898 987171

Editor: David C. Olsen

Cover Art: © 1991 KORG U.S.A. Used by Permission

Copyright © 1992 CPP/Belwin, Inc., Miami, FL 33014

— CONTENTS —

MOON RIVER

From The Paramount Pictures Production, "BREAKFAST AT TIFFANY'S"

Words by JOHNNY MERCER
Music by HENRY MANCINI

Moon River - 3 - 1

Moon River - 3 - 3

THE PINK PANTHER

Theme From The Mirisch-G&E Production, "THE PINK PANTHER", a United Artists Release

By HENRY MANCINI

The Pink Panther - 2 - 1

CHARADE

Theme Song From The Stanley Donen Production, A Universal Release

Words by JOHNNY MERCER
Music by HENRY MANCINI

Moderate Waltz

Charade - 4 - 1

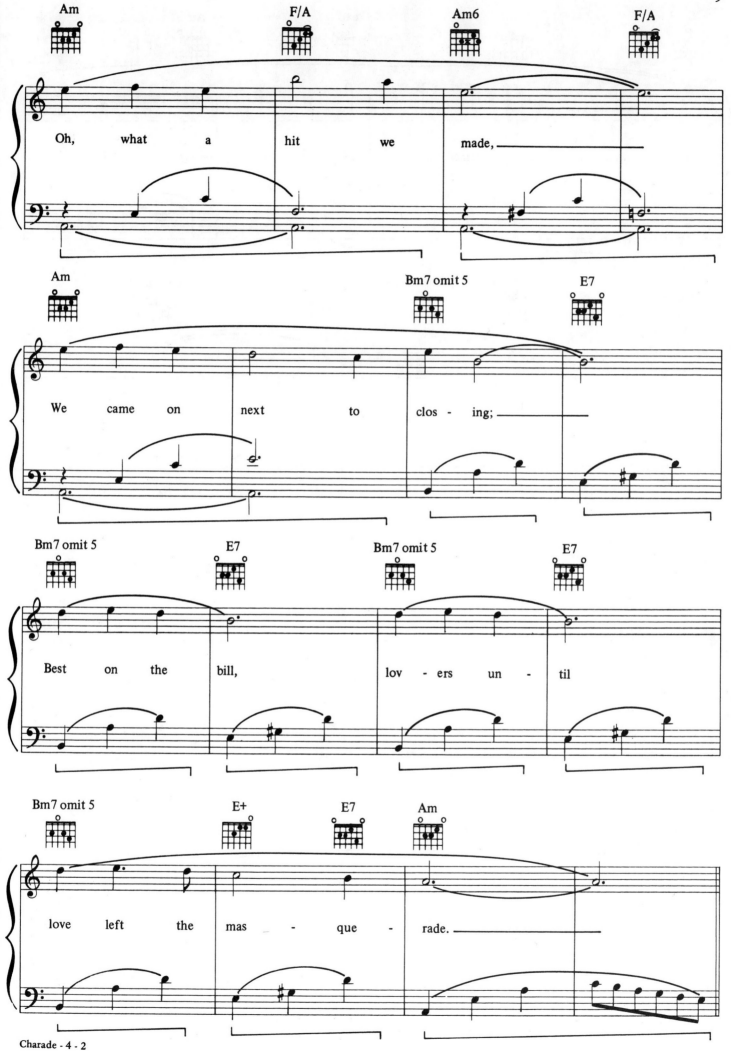

Charade - 4 - 2

DAYS OF WINE AND ROSES

From The Warner Bros. Picture "DAYS OF WINE AND ROSES"

Lyric by JOHNNY MERCER

Music by HENRY MANCINI

The DAYS _____ OF WINE AND ROS - ES _____

_____ Laugh and run a - way _____ Like a child at play, _____ Through the

mead-ow-land to - ward a clos-ing door, A door marked "Nev-er - more," That

Days Of Wine And Roses - 2 - 1

BABY ELEPHANT WALK

From The Paramount Pictures Production, "HATARI"

By HENRY MANCINI

Baby Elephant Walk - 4 - 1

Baby Elephant Walk - 4 - 4

DEAR HEART

Theme Song From The Warner Brothers Production

Words by JAY LIVINGSTON and RAY EVANS
Music by HENRY MANCINI

Dear Heart - 2 - 1

PETER GUNN

Theme Song from the Television Series

By HENRY MANCINI

Note: For four hands:
1st player take lower staff (𝄢) and
double the part an octave higher.
2nd player take upper staff (𝄞) and
double the part an octave higher.

Peter Gunn - 3 - 1

(R.H. ad lib. solo if desired)

loco

MR. LUCKY

Theme Song From The Television Series

Words by JAY LIVINGSTON and RAY EVANS
Music by HENRY MANCINI

Mr. Lucky - 3 - 1

CRAZY WORLD
(From Victor/Victoria)

Lyric by LESLIE BRICUSSE
Music by HENRY MANCINI

Crazy World - 4 - 1

ten - der; _____ gen - tle; _____ then

tem - p'ra - men - tal as a sum - mer storm. _____

Just when I be - lieve your heart's get - ting warm - er _____ you're

cold and you're cruel _____ and I like a fool try to

"LE JAZZ HOT!"
(From Victor/Victoria)

Lyric by LESLIE BRICUSSE
Music by HENRY MANCINI

Le Jazz Hot - 5 - 1

Easy tempo

Dm A7/E Dm C7 F A7

this mu - sic has.___ Be - fore they knew it, it was whiz - zin' 'round the world,

Dm A7/E Dm C7 F Eb7 D7

the world was read - y for a blue kind of mu - sic

Ad lib.
G9

and now they play it from Steam - boat Springs___ to La

colla voce   rit.

Swing 4
C7 Gm7/C C7 -5 +9 C7 Am/C Gm Db7 C7/6
No Chord

Paz.   Oh, ba - by,

f

32

won't you___ play me "Le Jazz Hot"___ may - be___ and

don't ev - er let_____ it end._____

I tell ya, friend, it's real - ly some - thin' to hear,___

I can't sit still when there's that rhy - thm near me.

Al - so,___ ba - by,___ "Le Jazz Hot"_ may be_ what's

hold - in' my soul___ to - geth - er.

Jazz Hot!

Don't know wheth - er it's morn - in' or night,___

on - ly know it's sound - in' right._____ So come on

Le Jazz Hot - 5 - 4

34

Le Jazz Hot - 5 - 5

YOU AND ME
(From Victor/Victoria)

Lyric by LESLIE BRICUSSE
Music by HENRY MANCINI

You and me, we're the kind of peo-ple oth-er peo-ple would like to be. Wan-d'ring free,

You And Me - 3 - 1

You And Me - 3 - 2

You And Me - 3 - 3

WHISTLING AWAY THE DARK

From The Blake Edwards Production, "DARLING LILI", A Paramount Release

Words by JOHNNY MERCER
Music by HENRY MANCINI

Whistling Away The Dark - 5 - 1

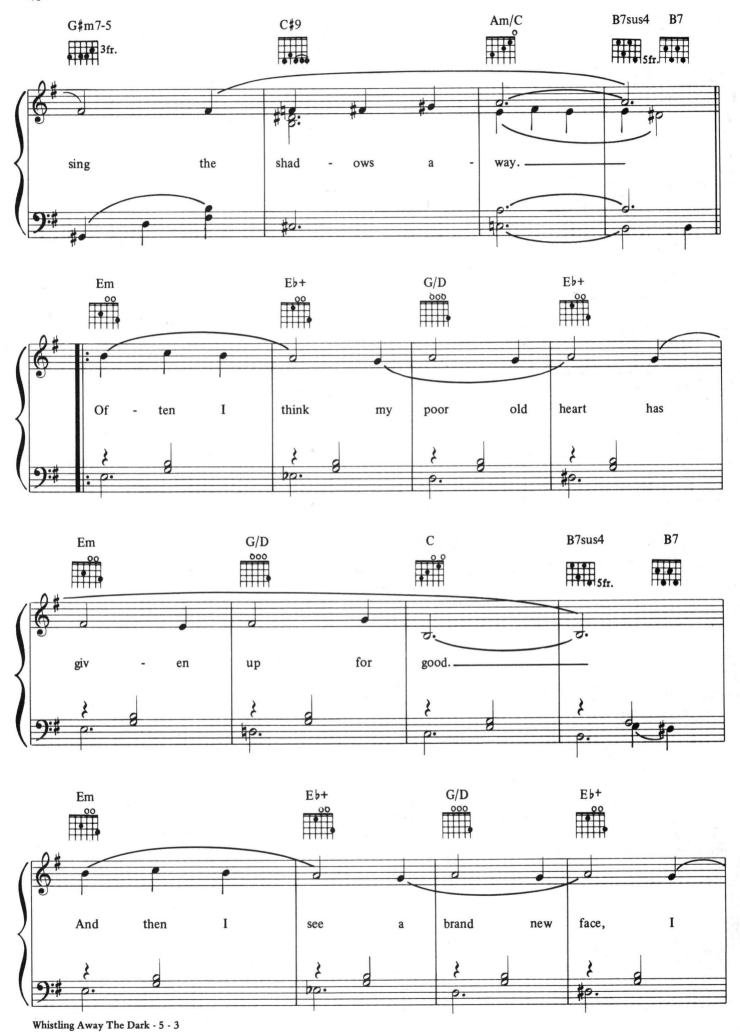

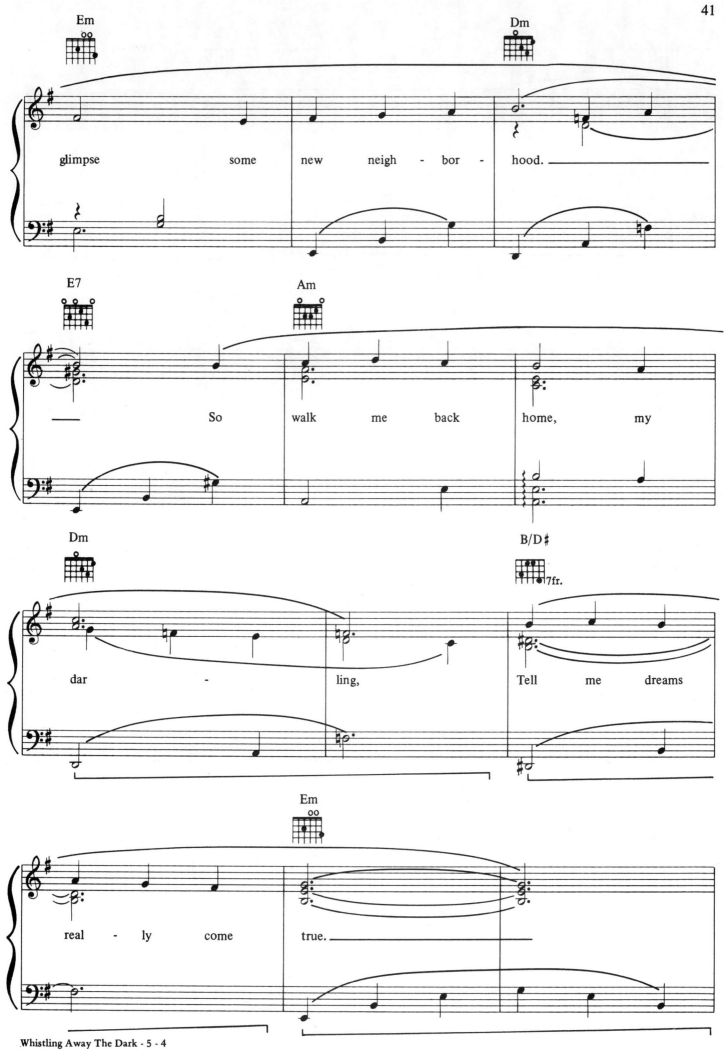

42

Whistling Away The Dark - 5 - 5

DARLING LILI

Theme Song From The Blake Edwards Production, A Paramount Release

Words by JOHNNY MERCER
Music by HENRY MANCINI

Darling Lili - 3 - 1

44

Darling Lili - 3 - 3

THE THORN BIRDS THEME

From The Warner Bros. T.V. Movie "THE THORN BIRDS"

By HENRY MANCINI

The Thorn Birds Theme - 2 - 1

The Thorn Birds Theme - 2 - 2

(Meggie's Theme)
ANYWHERE THE HEART GOES
(Song From The Thorn Birds)

Based on a Theme from the WARNER BROS. T.V. Movie, "THE THORN BIRDS"

Words by
WILL JENNINGS

Music by
HENRY MANCINI

You know I will fol-low an-y-where the heart goes. I will
go un-til I've known all life can be. _____

Anywhere The Heart Goes - 3 - 1

Love can hurt when you go   an-y-where the heart   goes.   Don't you

know   it is-n't eas-y   be-ing me?   I

hold   you in-side   where   my   love   nev-er   died,   and you will

al   -   ways   live   some-where   in   me.

Anywhere The Heart Goes - 3 - 2

SONG FROM "10"
(It's Easy To Say)

From The Geoffrey Productions, Inc. Picture, "10"

Lyric by ROBERT WELLS
Music by HENRY MANCINI

Lyrics:

It's eas-y to say it's o-ver. It's eas-y to say we're the best of friends. You walk a-

Song From "10" - 3 - 1

THE INSPECTOR CLOUSEAU THEME

From The Blake Edwards Production. "THE PINK PANTHER STRIKES AGAIN"

By HENRY MANCINI

Moderately (♩ = 138)

The Inspector Clouseau Theme - 3 - 1

The Inspector Clouseau Theme - 3 - 2

The Inspector Clouseau Theme - 3 - 3

BREAKFAST AT TIFFANY'S

Theme Song From The Paramount Pictures Production

By HENRY MANCINI

Moderato, not too slowly with expression

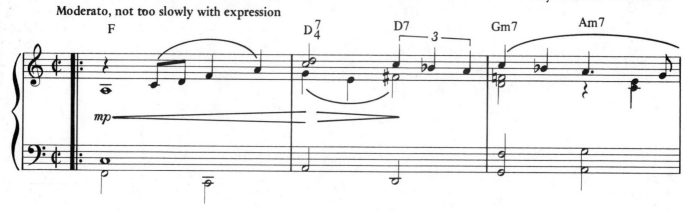

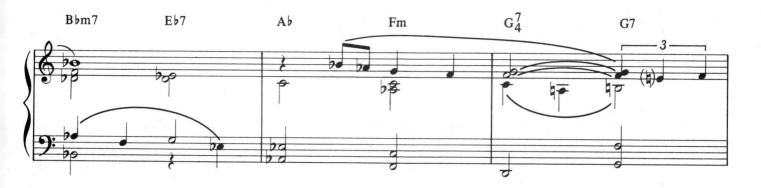

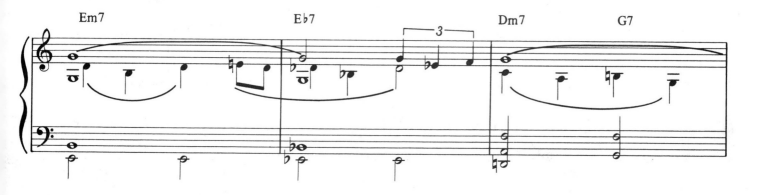

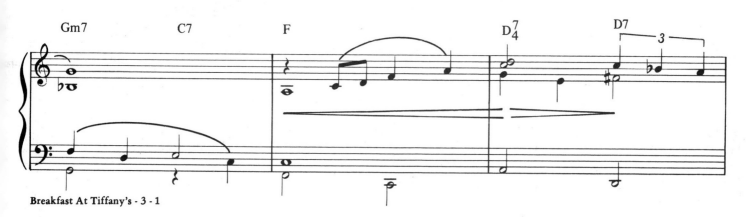

Breakfast At Tiffany's - 3 - 1

59

Breakfast At Tiffany's - 3 - 3

From The Columbia Motion Picture "THAT'S LIFE"

LIFE IN A LOOKING GLASS

Lyric by
LESLIE BRICUSSE

Music by
HENRY MANCINI

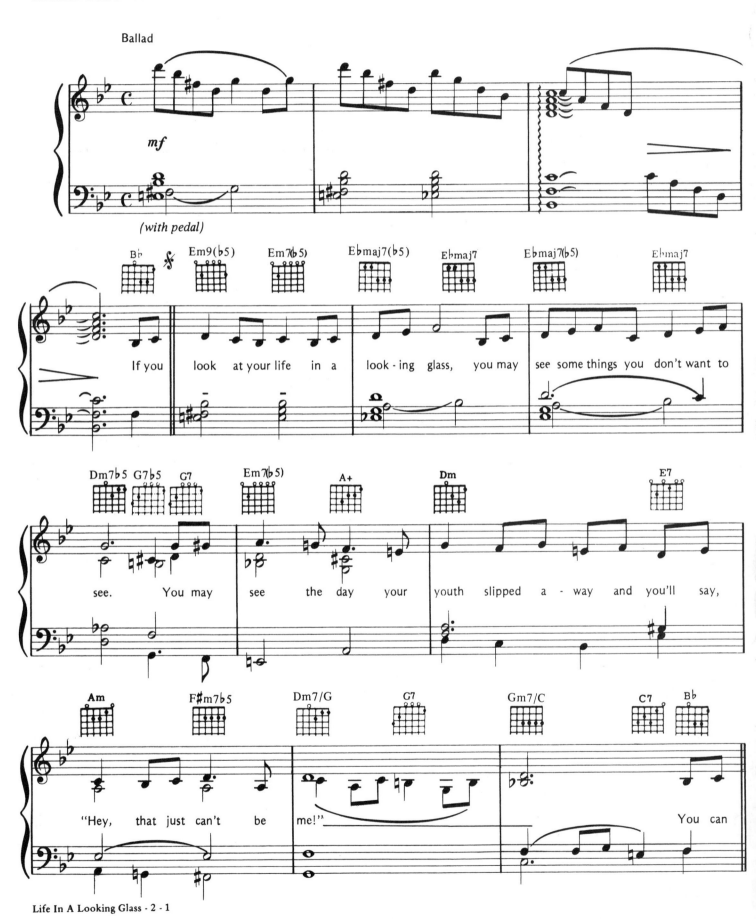

Life In A Looking Glass - 2 - 1

THE SWEETHEART TREE

From The Warner Brothers Production, "THE GREAT RACE"

Words by JOHNNY MERCER
Music by HENRY MANCINI

The Sweetheart Tree - 2 - 1

The Sweetheart Tree - 2 - 2